ROLLING IN THE AISLES

ROLLING IN THE AISLES

Murray Watts

MARC
The Children's Society

A royalty from each copy sold of this book goes to the work of the
Children's Society. For more information about the Society, see p.143.

Cartoons copyright © 1987 by Murray Watts

Cover cartoon by Norman Stone.

Copyright © 1987 by Murray Watts

First published 1987
Reprinted 1987

British Library Cataloguing in Publication Data

Watts, Murray   Rolling in the aisles.
  1. English wit and humour   2. Preaching
  I. Title
  828'.91402'080922   PN6175

ISBN 0-947697-65-9

Typeset in Britain for MARC, an imprint of Kingsway Publications,
Lottbridge Drove, Eastbourne, East Sussex BN23 6NT in Times Roman
by Nuprint Ltd, Harpenden, Herts AL5 4SE; covers printed by Creative
Print & Design, Unit 2/3 Saxon Way Trading Estate, Harmondsworth,
Middlesex UB7 0LW; text printed by Richard Clay Ltd, Bungay, Suffolk.

For Anita and Miranda

Acknowledgements

Rolling in the Aisles is a combination of my own collection of jokes and stories, made over many years; material collected by my friend, the late Canon David Watson; and a variety of anecdotes from different sources. I am particularly grateful to Anne Watson for graciously lending me David's card index of sermon illustrations. I would also like to thank Nigel Forde, Canon Raymond Hockley, John Whitehead, Derrick Gilbert, Peter Stacey, Rabbi Singer, Stephen Travis, and many others who have suggested material for this book.

Thanks are also due to Hodder & Stoughton, for permission to include a story told by Richard Wurmbrand in *In God's Underground*; to Tony Collins, Liz Gibson and other friends at MARC Europe for their patience in waiting for this manuscript; to Norman Stone, for a wonderful cover cartoon; and to Tom McCoulough, vicar of All Hallows Church, Sutton-on-Forest, for allowing me to work in the parish room during 1986.

Finally, I would like to thank Sir Harry Secombe for writing the foreword to this book. His personality and his gift for making people laugh have been a great inspiration to me.

Contents

Foreword
by Sir Harry Secombe

When I met Murray Watts, on a Highway programme in York, he told me that two of the greatest inspirations in his life were the Bible and the Goon Show! He explained that I had a lot to answer for... Well, learning of the work of Riding Lights Theatre Company, which has brought laughter and joy into churches and theatres all over the world, and reading a book like *Rolling in the Aisles*, I am delighted to be considered an influence.

Here is an anthology which does not laugh at religion but laughs about it, and discovers the truth through humour. The author sees the funny side of life from the perspective of faith. He has drawn his own cartoons, which add to the fun, and he has not been afraid to send himself up in a few of his personal reminiscences. I like that, because a sense of humour begins with not taking ourselves too seriously.

In a world that listens to too much bad news, I hope that a book like *Rolling in the Aisles* can lead to a better understanding of the good news. I also hope that it can further the work of the Children's Society. They deserve your support just as you deserve the pleasure of reading these stories.

Enjoy yourself with this book, as I did.

Yours most sincerely,

Harry Secombe

Introduction

I began writing this book in the parish room of All Hallows Church, Sutton-on-Forest, only a few yards away from the pulpit which was once occupied by the craziest vicar in English history, Laurence Sterne. A book of funny stories is hardly a worthy descendant of his surreal masterpiece *Tristram Shandy*, but at least I can borrow a sentiment from his introduction: 'As we jog on, either laugh with me, or at me, or in short, do anything—only keep your temper.'

These stories are to delight and amuse; perhaps to teach; but they are never meant to offend. If they do, or if the very idea of religious humour is troubling, I can only quote another ecclesiastical wit, the nineteenth-century cleric, Sydney Smith: 'You must not think me necessarily foolish because I am facetious. Nor will I consider you necessarily wise because you are grave.' Telling a funny story can be a way of expressing faith, just as preaching a very serious sermon, without light or joy, may be the product of unbelief.

The chapter divisions in *Rolling in the Aisles* are really for the fun of bedtime reading, but a subject like 'prayer' is covered in many different areas of the book. This is why I have numbered the stories and included an index for general reference. As for the little introductions to each chapter, I have usually taken stories from my own experience, or from my family's, to explain the theme. I have also numbered these whenever I thought they might be relevant to speakers searching for an illustration.

Children are the world's greatest resource of humour. *Rolling in the Aisles* begins with children, and it also ends with a few words abqut The Children's Society, which has a special relationship with this book. I hope that, apart from giving a little practical help, *Rolling in the Aisles* will join forces with other books of religious humour and become a subversive influence on all forms of piety which prevent us from becoming like little children, humble and ready to laugh.

Murray Watts
York

SUFFER
THE LITTLE
CHILDREN

1 My neighbour's four-year-old son was asked to say grace. He closed his eyes, put his hands together, and in perfect innocence prayed:

'Give us the food for Christ's sake, Amen.'

2 On another occasion, I was at a church service with members of my family. My aunt had been away from church for a while and she had two envelopes for the collection plate. She gave one to her four-year-old grandson. When the plate came to her, he whispered,

'It's all right, Gran, I've paid for you.'

Here are a few more inspirational moments from children. Some of them have happened, like the stories above; others, no doubt, will happen before very long.

3 A minister, arriving as a visiting speaker to a neighbouring church, decided to take a very informal approach with the children. Word had reached him of the strict and pious atmosphere of the Sunday school, and he decided he would introduce a refreshing change of approach. Sitting on the edge of a desk, wearing an open-neck shirt, he leaned confidentially towards the children.

'Can anyone tell me,' he asked them, 'what is small, grey, eats nuts and has a large bushy tail?'

There was a long silence, then one small boy put up his hand and said,

'I know the answer should be Jesus, but it sounds like a squirrel to me.'

4 There was a blinding flash of lightning and Emily, aged five, rushed into the house, shouting:

'Mummy, Mummy, God has just taken my picture!'

5 A little boy was kneeling beside his bed with his mother and grandmother and softly saying his prayers:

'Dear God, please bless Mummy and Daddy and all the family and please give me a good night's sleep.' Suddenly he looked up and shouted: 'AND DON'T FORGET TO GIVE ME A TRANSFORMER FOR MY BIRTHDAY!!'

'There's no need to shout like that,' said his mother, 'God isn't deaf.'

'No,' said the little boy, 'but Grandma is.'

6 During a long and very boring sermon, a small but distinct voice could be heard at the back of the church, asking:

'Mummy, is it *still* Sunday?'

7 A family was entertaining some pious friends for dinner. The hostess, keen to show that they upheld Christian standards in their own home, asked her five-year-old son to say grace. He looked blank. There was an awkward pause, followed by a reassuring smile from the boy's mother.

'Well, darling, just say what Daddy said at breakfast this morning.'

Obediently, the boy repeated, 'Oh God, we've got those awful people coming for dinner tonight.'

8 Written by a child in a school essay, after visiting a church in Melton Mowbray:

'The difference between the Church of England and the Methodist Church is that the Methodist Church has double glazing.'

(*Reported in the* Church Times)

9 The junior form was doing a project on the Creation. George, aged seven, wrote:

'God made the first man and called him *Adam*. Then God made the first woman and called her *Madam*.'

10 Little girl: Is it true that we come from dust and go to dust?
Mother: Yes, the Bible says so.
Little girl: In that case, lots of people are either coming or going under my bed.

11 The headmaster made an impromptu visit to a junior classroom. The pupils sweated with fear as he fired questions, one after another, which they failed to answer.

'Who made the world?' he asked sternly. There was silence.

'I said, who made the world?' The headmaster raised his voice threateningly.

'Children,' he bent over the front row, 'I want to know who made the world.'

A small boy blurted out in terror, 'Oh sir, please sir, it wasn't me!'

12 During a family communion service at a church in York two little boys went up to the altar rail with their parents. As the minister passed along the line, giving bread to the adults and blessing the children, one little boy looked hungrily at the loaf. His brother whispered,

'Go on, give him a bit, it's his birthday!'

13 Argument in a playground:

First Boy: My Daddy is a teacher and makes me clever for nothing!

Second Boy: My Daddy is a doctor and makes me healthy for nothing!

Third Boy: My Daddy is a vicar and makes me good for nothing!

14 'God doesn't love me,' cried the little girl.

'Don't be silly,' said her father, 'of course he does!'

She refused to be comforted. 'I know he doesn't because I tried him with a daisy.'

15 Asked to write what he knew about Martin Luther, a schoolboy summed up the life of the great reformer in these words:

'Martin Luther was originally a German monk who had a diet of worms, after which he said, "I can take no other course."'

16 From a schoolgirl's essay:
'Armistice was signed on November 11th, 1918, and since then we have had two minutes of peace every year.'

17 'Daddy, what's that?' said the little boy, looking up from their pew at the memorial plaque on the wall.

'That's in memory of all the brave men who died in the services.'

The little boy scanned the long list of names and asked: 'Did they die in the morning or evening services?'

18
Little Girl:	Mummy, who made me?
Mother:	God did.
Little Girl:	Who made you?
Mother:	God did.
Little Girl:	Who made Grandma?
Mother:	God did.
	PAUSE.
Little Girl:	He's improved a lot since he made Grandma.

19 Teacher: Who was most unhappy when the Prodigal Son came home?

Pupil: The fatted calf.

20 A schoolboy was set the task of translating and explaining the motto 'Dieu et mon droit', seen beneath the Royal arms of Great Britain. This was his interpretation:

'Queen Elizabeth I was about to step in a muddy puddle when Sir Walter Raleigh stepped forward and covered it with his cloak. The Queen stepped over safely but then turned to Raleigh and said,

"I am afraid that I have spoiled your cloak."

'Raleigh replied: "My God! You're right!"'

21 Little girl: Does God make lions, Mummy?

Mother: Yes, dear.

Little girl: But isn't he *frightened* to?

22 Sunday school teacher: What does the story of Goliath teach us?

Boy: To duck.

23 Soon after the Dead Sea Scrolls were discovered, a small boy was listening to the radio. He looked at his father anxiously:

'I hope they haven't found any more commandments.'

24
Teacher:	What are you drawing, Susan?
Susan:	A picture of Jesus.
Teacher:	But no one knows what Jesus looked like.
Susan:	They will when I've finished.

25 Two little girls tiptoed past their grandmother.
'Why is Granny always reading the Bible?' asked Kate.

'Ssh!' whispered Lizzie, 'we mustn't disturb her! She's cramming for her finals.'

THE GOOD,
THE BAD
AND
THE BORING

26 I remember David Watson preaching on the intimacy of prayer. He illustrated this by pointing to the reredos in St Michael-le-Belfrey Church, where the Lord's Prayer is written in full. The sign-writer had difficulty getting each phrase onto a separate line, so the Lord's Prayer begins—beautifully and simply—'Our Father which art in heaven, hallo.'

The sermons in this chapter range from the never-to-be-forgotten, to the easily-forgotten, to the best-forgotten.

27 A curate had suffered a very difficult working relationship with his vicar over the three years of his first curacy. At last, it was time for him to leave. No more would he have to endure the stubbornness and pedantry of this impossible man. He preached his final sermon to the congregation on the text, 'Abide ye here with the ass, and I will go yonder.'

28 A bishop visited a church in his diocese. Only three people turned up to hear him preach. He asked the rector,

'Did you give notice of my visit?'

'No,' replied the rector, 'but the word seems to have got round.'

29 A visiting preacher stood at the door of the church after the service, shaking hands with one person after another who thanked him for his sermon. 'A wonderful message', 'Marvellous', 'A powerful word', 'Tremendously helpful'.

The speaker was deeply flattered. Then a rather strange-looking man came up to him, muttering, 'Talked too long!' He decided to ignore this and continued shaking hands with members of the congregation who thanked him warmly. Then the strange little man reappeared. 'Load of nonsense!'

The speaker tried to take no notice, but the man kept rejoining the queue and each time he came up to the speaker he would complain about something different: 'Didn't understand a word!', 'Irrelevant', 'Bored to tears!'

Finally, the visiting preacher could stand it no longer.

'Who is that man?' he asked the vicar.

'Oh don't worry about him,' came the reassuring reply. 'He's a little simple in the head. He just spends all his time repeating what everyone else says.'

30 Preacher to congregation:
'My job is to preach and your job is to listen. If you finish your job before I've finished mine, please keep quiet.'

31 A visiting preacher was aware that he had overstepped the mark with his 45-minute sermon.

'I'm so sorry,' he explained to the verger, 'but there wasn't a clock in front of me', to which the verger replied, 'No, but there was a calendar behind you.'

32 C H Spurgeon once asked a student for the ministry to preach an impromptu sermon. The result merits an entry in the *Guinness Book of Records* for the shortest sermon ever. Appropriately, it was on the subject of Zacchaeus, and this is how it went:

'First, Zacchaeus was a man of very small stature; so am I. Second, Zacchaeus was very much up a tree; so am I. Third, Zacchaeus made haste and came down; so will I.' With that, the student sat down to shouts of 'More, more!' from his fellows.

'No,' said Spurgeon, 'he could not improve upon that if he tried.'

33 A pastor fell out with his church. After bitter arguments, he was forced to leave and take up a job as a prison chaplain. He preached his last sermon at the church on John 14:1: 'I go to prepare a place for you.'

34 The local minister preached a splendid sermon on creation. He spoke eloquently of the natural world.

'Why,' he stretched out his arms, 'every blade of grass can preach a sermon!'

Later, a parishioner saw him mowing his lawn and shouted, 'That's right, minister, keep your sermons short!'

35 Someone had stolen the vicar's bike. He felt sure that one of his parishioners was the thief, so he decided to preach a sermon on the Ten Commandments. When he came to 'Thou shalt not steal', he made a great deal of the commandment, preaching eloquently about the scourge of theft and the collapse of standards in our society, but when he came to the commandment 'Thou shalt not commit adultery', he suddenly remembered where he'd left his bike.

36 A preacher was notoriously boring. One Sunday, the verger tried a little experiment to liven up the sermon—he laced the vicar's water with gin. The sermon that followed was remarkable. It was funny, down-to-earth, full of neat illustrations, hard-hitting and spiritually enlightening. The parishioners were astonished and the verger was jubilant.

The next Sunday, he stepped up the gin in the water and another sensational sermon followed, even more powerful than the last.

On the third Sunday, the bishop was visiting the church so, in honour of this occasion, the verger put nine-tenths gin to one-tenth water. The vicar excelled himself preaching on the story of Daniel in the Lion's Den. The pulpit shook as he paced up and down, he acted the parts, he laughed, he cried, he shouted, he whispered, he touched the hearts of his congregation, he fired their enthusiasm, he inspired them to follow Daniel's example. After the service, the bishop shook the vicar's hand warmly.

'A very good sermon,' he told him, 'but there's only one small point. God sent an angel to shut the mouths of the lions, Daniel didn't "zap them between the eyes and strew their brains across the walls like spaghetti."'

37 The besetting sin of a young Presbyterian minister was conceit. He frequently boasted in public that all the time he needed to prepare his sermons was the few moments that it took him to walk to church from his manse next door. The elders had the perfect remedy. They bought him a new manse five miles away.

38 A vicar was on holiday when his house was flooded. All his sermons were kept in the basement and the first question he asked his son, who had gone in to investigate the damage, was: 'Are my sermons wet?'

'No, Dad,' came the inevitable reply, 'they're as dry as ever.'

39 George Whitefield, the great eighteenth-century preacher, told a story about the most famous actor of his day, David Garrick.

A preacher asked him, 'How is it that you actors are able, on the stage, to produce so great an effect with fiction; whilst we preachers, in the pulpit, obtain such a small result with the facts?'

Garrick replied, 'I suppose it is because we present fiction as though it were fact, whilst you, too often, offer facts as though they were fiction.'

40 A Victorian preacher stood up in a Temperance Hall and graphically illustrated the perils of alcohol. He took out a live worm from a tin of fisherman's bait and dropped it into a glass of whisky. The worm expired and the preacher triumphantly asked,

'Now, what does that teach us?'

A heckler shouted: 'If you've got worms, drink whisky.'

41 The N'toto people had been Christians for many years when they were visited by a western theologian, famous for his radical views. He was welcomed by the chief, who showed him round the tribal lands, pointing out the vast numbers of pigs, goats and chickens which the N'toto people possessed. Before he was due to leave, the chief asked the theologian to preach a sermon to the tribe. The theologian agreed, but he was worried about the language barrier. The chief assured him that, although the people could not speak English, they could understand it, so the theologian climbed onto a tree stump and addressed the huge crowd which had gathered.

'Christianity,' he began, 'is really one of many tribal myths.'

'Kabola! Kabola!' shouted the people, enthusiastically.

'As a matter of fact, it is doubtful if the resurrection ever happened as a historical event.'

'Kabola! Kabola!' chanted the crowd.

The theologian was delighted with the warm reception. 'I'm so glad that you understand my views better than many people in the West. You see, God is really in all of us and Jesus was just an example of that.'

'Kabola! Kabola!' cheered the crowd.

The theologian went on to speak about the impossibility of miracles, the unreliability of the gospels, and concluded his sermon by saying, 'It is doubtful whether God himself, in the sense of the word, exists at all.'

'Kabola! Kabola!' the crowd roared.

The theologian stepped down, gratified to be such a success with the N'toto tribe.

'Before you go,' said the chief, 'let me show you our herd of cattle, but be careful not to tread in the Kabola.'

42 Parishioner: Your sermon was too long by half.
Preacher: Ah, well, brother, remember that we are admonished to declare the milk of the Word.
Parishioner: Make it condensed milk next time.

THE
ERROR
OF OUR
WAYS

43 Many years ago, a friend of mine was invited to tea by the Archbishop of York, then Dr Donald Coggan. She was nervous of meeting such an eminent churchman and quite unsure how to address him. Should it be 'Your Grace', 'Archbishop', or simply 'Dr Coggan'? Her nerves got the better of her for, when it came to it, she called him 'Arch-Coggan'.

Slips of the tongue can also produce some interesting variations on the Bible. In the early days of Riding Lights Theatre Company, I was the narrator in a street theatre performance of the story of David and Goliath. Liberal theologians would have appreciated my version. I shouted to the crowd: 'And so the Israelites saw that God was dead and Goliath was on their side.'

As for misprints, the possibilities are endless. One of the most embarrassing (and difficult) instructions to follow was on my own wedding service sheet. The rubric ran: 'At this point the bridegroom takes the bride's hind in his.'

Here is a brief catalogue of verbal and literary disasters.

44 Mrs Burton has no clothes. She has not had any for a year. Clergy have been visiting her.
(From a report filed by a DHSS Care Officer)

45 Our photograph shows Mr and Mrs H J Hill leaping the Hurlingham Church Hall yesterday after the marriage ceremony.

(Buenos Aires Herald)

46 Church member to minister:
'You'll never know what your sermon meant to me. It was like water to a drowning man!'

47 Violence has no place in our society. Anyone who preaches violence should be shot like a dog.
(Heard on KGO Radio, San Francisco)

48 'This is the House of God
These are the gates of Heaven.'
These doors are locked in winter.
(Notice outside a church in Cheshire)

49 Yours must be a soul-destroying job, vicar.
(Overheard at a party)

50 Mr Bradfield was elected and has accepted the office of People's Churchwarden. We could not get a better man.

(Parish magazine)

51 A bishop received an ambiguous letter from one of his clergymen:
'Dear Bishop,
    I regret to inform you that my wife has died. Could you please send me a substitute for the weekend?'

52 There is an epitaph for an eighteenth-century lady in York Minster. It lists about twenty of the virtues she possessed and then adds: 'For the rest of her virtues, see the Gentleman's Magazine of May 1763.'

53 The vicar is on holiday until the 27th. Local clergy will be celebrating on the Sundays when he is away.
(Parish magazine of All Saints, Kings Langley)

54 A printer's error on a service sheet changed 'Our God reigns' into 'Our God resigns'.

(Told by Richard Hare, Bishop of Pontefract)

55 One Sunday morning, a visiting preacher arrived at a small village chapel in County Durham. Not knowing that the names of all visiting preachers were hung on a special noticeboard, he was dismayed to hear the steward announce calmly, 'Our preacher for this evening is hanging in the vestibule.'

(Told by John Whitehead)

56 Are you 45 and getting nowhere? Why not consider the Christian ministry?

(Advert in a United Reformed Church)

57 'Vicar,' beamed the old lady appreciatively, 'we didn't know what sin was until you came to this parish.'

A
WORD
IN
SEASON

58 I remember a preacher who used to come to our beach in Hoylake, where I was born, to lead seaside missions. He was a great big man, once a professional boxer, and his party trick was to balance two small children on each of his outstretched arms. He was the Desperate Dan of the Christian ministry. Any moment I expected him to rip a Bible commentary in half or eat a cow pie with a text on it.

I did hear, many years later, of one occasion when this man's incredible physique came in handy at an evangelistic tent meeting. Every time he mentioned the Bible, a heckler shouted, 'I don't believe it!' 'Rubbish!' 'Myths!' 'Don't believe a word of it!'

Finally, the huge preacher lost patience, seized the man by the scruff of the neck and said: 'In the book of Proverbs it says, "The wringing of the nose bringeth forth blood," and if you don't believe it, I'll show you!!'

Everyone dreams of having the right words at the right moment, but I must admit I was floored by this conversation:

59 I was talking to members of the audience after a street-theatre performance in a pub car park.

'Oh, I know all about Jesus and his miracles,' said one person. His hand swept through the air. 'Oh, yes. Turning bricks into water. Things like that.'

I tentatively suggested that, generally speaking, Jesus performed rather more *useful* miracles than turning bricks into water. 'I will dissolve this temple in three days' somehow didn't sound right.

'Oh, well,' his friend interrupted, 'the Bible's full of contradictions anyway.'

'Which ones had you in mind?' I asked.

'Well, the book of Proverbs, for a start: "Many hands make light work" and "Too many cooks spoil the broth."'

Some other memorable responses follow:

60 A man snubbed the local vicar at a cocktail party. 'The church is full of hypocrites!'

'Why don't you join,' suggested the vicar, 'one more won't make any difference.'

61 Preacher: Can everyone hear me at the back?
Voice from
the back: Yes, but I wouldn't mind changing seats with someone who can't.

62 An aggressive atheist accosted a preacher.
'You believe in eternal life?' The preacher had no time to reply. 'Well, it's a load of rubbish!' shouted the atheist, with a stream of invective. 'I believe in science, evolution, survival of the fittest, and when we die, that's it! Caput! Finito!' He laboured his point tirelessly. 'Eternal life, ha!!' he spat, as his monologue reached its climax, 'Trash! When I die I am utterly convinced that will be the end of me!'

'Thank God for that,' said the preacher.

63 An international team of scientists worked for many years to develop a computer which could assess the evidence for the existence of God with mathematical precision. At last the great day came and, at a ceremony attended by Nobel prizewinners and the leaders of all the main churches, the computer was switched on and fed the ultimate question: 'Is there a God?'

Lights flashed, machinery hummed, a billion impulses raced through the computer's brain. Out came the reply:

'There is now.'

64 A woman went up to a highly respected clergyman and asked him, 'How would you cope with a serious drink problem?'

He replied, 'With a corkscrew, madam.'

65
Bishop:	Who is it that sees and hears all we do, and before whom even I am but as a crushed worm?
Page:	The Missus, my Lord.

(*Punch* cartoon, 1880)

66 A vicar was leaving his parish and paid a farewell visit to an elderly parishioner. The old man shook the vicar's hand warmly.

'Your successor won't be as good as you,' he assured him.

'Nonsense,' said the vicar, flattered.

'No, really,' said his parishioner, 'I've been here under five vicars, and each new one has been worse than the last.'

67 A film star turned up for her show-biz wedding wearing a topless mini dress. The vicar refused to allow her into the church.

She was furious, shouting: 'I have a divine right!'

To which the vicar replied, 'You've got a divine left as well, but you're not coming in here.'

68 The prison chaplain shook hands solemnly with one of the prisoners. After inquiring about his health and his family, he concluded: 'I hope I will never see you here again, Kenny.'

'Father,' replied Kenny, with absolute conviction, 'anyone who has heard you preach will not want to come here again.'

69 A story is told of Archbishop Thompson of York. He came across three men arguing over a fine copper kettle.

'Dear me,' he said, 'whatever's the matter?'

'Well, tha knows, reverence,' explained the eldest, ''tis

like this. Whoever can tell biggest lie, gets yon copper kettle.'

The archbishop was shocked. 'Why,' he exclaimed, 'I don't know how you could countenance such a thing. I have never told a lie in my whole life!'

The men were impressed. 'Tha canst 'ave this kettle then, for tha's biggest liar of all!'

70 A woman told Archbishop Temple about the miraculous escape of her aunt from certain death. Apparently, her aunt was about to leave on a sea voyage when she had a terrifying dream—the boat sank with all hands on board. She had the same dream twice and abandoned her trip. True to her premonition, the vessel sank with a terrible loss of life.

'Now don't you consider, Archbishop,' said the woman, 'that it was a remarkable interposition of providence to save my aunt?'

'Well, ma'am,' replied Temple, 'as I don't know your aunt, I can't say.'

71 In the last century, a young sailor and a famous preacher (reputedly C H Spurgeon) were sitting opposite each other in a railway carriage. The sailor took his pipe out of his pocket and, aware of the preacher's stern gaze, rather nervously began to stuff it with tobacco. Eventually, the preacher leaned forward.

'Excuse me,' he said, in a voice that made people tremble in their pews, 'but haven't you got a conscience about smoking your pipe?'

'Er, well—yes, I have, as a matter of fact,' said the sailor, apologetically, and put the pipe back into his pocket.

A few minutes later, the sailor was astonished to see the preacher take a pipe out of his pocket, stuff it with tobacco and light it.

'Excuse me, sir,' said the sailor, deeply disturbed, 'but haven't *you* got a conscience about smoking *your* pipe?'

'No,' said the preacher, puffing contentedly, 'none at all.'

72 The vicar stormed into the vestry and flung his sermon notes on the table.

'Today,' he shouted to the verger, 'I have preached to a congregation of asses!'

The verger nodded. 'So that was why you kept on calling them "beloved brethren."'

73 A bishop tells how he visited a church and talked to a man who had been a churchwarden for forty years.

'You must have seen some changes in the church during your forty years.'

'Yes, I have,' replied the churchwarden, 'and I have opposed every single one of them!'

(Told by Richard Hare, Bishop of Pontefract)

74 Many years ago, a woman was at a mission meeting led by the preacher Gipsy Smith. She wrote to him afterwards: 'Dear Sir, I feel that God is calling me to preach the Gospel. The trouble is, I have twelve children. What shall I do?'

Gipsy Smith replied: 'Dear Madam, I am delighted to hear that God has called you to preach the Gospel. I am even more delighted to hear that he has provided you with a congregation.'

75 Lilian Bayliss, founder of the Old Vic and one of the greatest theatrical managers ever, was a devoutly religious woman. She had many friends in the church, as well as in the theatre, and on one occasion she was greeted by a bishop in a dressing room. They were alone and embraced, first warmly and then almost passionately, when suddenly there was a knock on the door.

'Oh, Bishop,' exclaimed Lilian, 'The Holy Ghost. Just in time!'

76 The vicar shook hands with his parishioners and watched them hurry off down the road to The Pig and Whistle.

'Why is there a headlong rush for the pub after evensong?' he asked.

'Well,' replied the curate, 'I suppose you could call it the "thirst after righteousness."'

77 The dean of a Cambridge college caught a student climbing over the college wall after lock-up.

'Oh God!' said the student.

'No,' replied the dean, 'just his accredited representative.'

78 A lady asked the Reverend Charles Simeon if a Christian should always be talking about religion.

'No, no,' exclaimed the great preacher. 'Let your speech be seasoned with salt—*seasoned* with salt, madam, not a whole mouthful!'

79 Dr D W L Watkinson was renowned for his quick replies. One day, during a stay at a Methodist conference, he arrived very late for breakfast. His fellow ministers reminded him that John Wesley had risen at 4.00 am every morning.

'I would too,' said Dr Watkinson, 'if I were married to Wesley's wife.'

80 King Herod had imprisoned the prophet John the Baptist for preaching against his adulterous marriage. Yet, according to the Bible, he was reluctant to do away with this dissident voice in his kingdom altogether, and kept him in prison. Then follows one of the most gruesome stories in the Bible when Herod, infatuated by the dancing of Salome, promises her 'anything, even to the half of my kingdom'. Goaded by her mother, she requests the head of John the Baptist on a platter. Herod's dilemma seems an impossible one, but not according to a missionary who tells of a brilliant and typically African solution to the problem. When asking one of her students what he would have said in Herod's place, she received the answer: 'I would have said that the Baptist's head belonged to the half of the kingdom I did not promise.'

81 Two men were discussing religion. One man said, 'I don't have anything to do with things I don't understand.'

'Have you had your breakfast this morning?' asked the other.

'Yes,' said the first, 'but what's that got to do with religion?'

'Did you have any butter on your toast?' persisted his friend.

'Yes,' replied the man, increasingly bewildered.

'Well, can you tell me how a black and white cow eating green grass can make white milk that makes yellow butter?'

'No, I can't,' admitted the sceptic.

'Well,' his friend advised, 'I wouldn't have anything to do with breakfast then.'

82 Samuel Johnson's epic struggle to finish his dictionary is legendary. His biographer, James Boswell, describes the final delivery to the publisher.

'When the messenger carried the last sheet to Miller and returned, Johnson asked him, "Well, what did he say?"

"Sir," answered the messenger, "he said, 'Thank God I have done with him!'"

"I am glad," replied Johnson with a smile, "that he thanks God for anything."'

83 A poster read: 'God is dead'—Nietzche.
The graffiti underneath read: 'Nietzche is dead'—God.

MONEY MATTERS

84 Our cheque books have more to do with Heaven and Hell than our hymn books.

(Helmut Thielicke)

It's a worrying thought. When did we ever clutch our hymn books with moist palms? Would we go berserk with anxiety and ring the police if we lost one copy of Ancient and Modern?

Learning to handle money responsibly is about as difficult as trying to say the phrase 'where moth and rust doth corrupt' in a hurry.

Here are seven stories on a very tricky subject.

85

| First man: | I didn't see you at church on the Sabbath. |
| Second man: | I noticed that when I was taking the collection. |

86 A vicar was trying to persuade a millionaire to support the Church Steeple Fund. He took him inside the tower and pointed to the cracks in the walls. Just then, a piece of masonry dislodged itself and struck the man a glancing blow.

'Good grief,' he said, rubbing his head, 'I see what you mean, here's a cheque for £100.'

'Go on, Lord,' shouted the vicar, 'hit him again!'

87 A couple had just got married. The clergyman shook hands with the bride, but the husband stuck his hands deep into his pockets. The clergyman held out his hand.

'Hang on! Hang on!' said the bridegroom, 'can't you see I'm getting the money out as fast as I can?'

88 A pastor was trying to cheer up his gloomy congregation: 'In these days of escalating inflation, isn't it good to know that the wages of sin remain just the same?'

89 Man calling at the vicarage: Any old clothes, Lady?
Vicar's wife: No, thank you, I have all I can afford at present.

AMEN

90 Lazarus, the beggar, knocked on the door of his wealthy neighbour, Dives. It was 6.30 am and Dives was furious. 'How dare you wake me up so early?'

'Listen', said Lazarus, 'I don't tell you how to run your business, so don't you tell me how to run mine.'

91 A very rich man died. He was famous for his magnificent collection of art treasures, antiques and silver. After the funeral, a journalist whispered to the vicar, 'How much did he leave?'

'Everything,' whispered the vicar.

SECRET VICES

92 A relative of mine was at an exclusive girls' boarding school. Although it was the 'permissive sixties', the housemistress managed to preserve the morality of a bygone age. When the girls saw a man running round the garden with no trousers on, they dashed into her sitting room: 'Miss Mckay, Miss Mckay, there's a *man* in the garden and he's only wearing a *shirt*!'

'WHAT??' bellowed the stunned housemistress, 'no *jacket*?'

What is 'permissible' may depend upon our perspective— or so the sociologists tell us. Yet, despite the widespread influence of the 'permissive society', the clergy have some- how been missed out. They are not really permitted any vices or sins, at least not in public, and so they have to go to considerable lengths . . .

93 Seamus staggered out of the pub and bumped into a passing nun.

'Now will you leave the demon drink alone?' scolded the nun.

'To be sure and why should that be?' asked Seamus, ''Tis the very elixir of life.'

'It's a terrible shame,' continued the nun, 'that a fine young boy like you, that should be the pride and joy of your mother's grey hairs, would go down to the grave before her.'

'Oh, no, Sister,' protested Seamus, 'a little drink never did a man no harm.'

'Will you not give over now,' said the nun, 'will the demon drink be the death of you then?'

'Now why should you call it the demon drink,' said Seamus, brazenly, 'have you ever tasted the stuff?'

'And why would I be doing such a terrible thing as that, my child,' cried the nun. 'Will you have me forsake my holy vows of temperance?'

'Go on, Sister,' persisted Seamus, 'it cannot be holy or righteous to condemn something which you know nothing about. I'll get you a drop and you can judge for yourself. What will you have?'

'Well,' said the nun, faltering, 'perhaps you're right, I shouldn't make the judgement so hastily after all.'

'Whisky? Brandy? Gin?' asked Seamus, pushing open the door of the pub.

'Oh now, I'm surely doing a terrible wrong thing,' said the nun, beginning to leave.

'Go on,' said Seamus, putting a hand on her shoulder, 'have a go!'

'Well, perhaps I should try a drop or two of that gin, only bring it to me in a teacup. It would be a shameful thing for a nun to be seen tasting liquor outside a public house.'

'Right,' said Seamus, going up to the bar. 'Pour me a gin, please, but put it in a teacup.'

'Good grief,' said the landlord, 'It's that alcoholic nun again.'

94 Would the member of the congregation who wrote in a hymn book last Sunday, 'Five pounds each way Fanciful Lad on Wednesday' kindly remove the page, as the vicar found it most misleading.

(Announcement in a Yorkshire church)

95 A vicar invited a curate and a bishop back to his house after the garden fête. He offered them drinks, and the bishop gratefully accepted a double whisky. Turning to the curate, he asked: 'Would you like a little drop of something?'

'Certainly not!' was the self-righteous response, 'I'd rather commit adultery.'

'Oh,' said the bishop, handing back his glass. 'I didn't know there was a choice.'

96 A Methodist minister had a secret vice—he loved a tipple of cherry brandy. Of course, it was impossible for him to admit this weakness to a congregation who were strictly teetotal, and some wicked friends decided to exploit his dilemma. They offered him a whole crate of cherry brandy on condition that the gift was publicly acknowledged in the parish magazine. To their amazement, the minister gladly accepted. Next Sunday the notice duly appeared: 'The minister would like to thank his friends for the generous gift of fruit and the spirit in which it was given.'

97 Seventy per cent of all bishops take *The Times*. The other thirty per cent pay for it.

98 A little old lady was given two parrots. She wanted to know which was the male and which was the female, so she decided to lay a cloth over the cage and study them secretly through a spy-hole. She watched the parrots for several hours until one of them looked round nervously, sidled along the perch and gave the other one a quick peck on the cheek. The male had been identified. She whipped off the cloth, seized the parrot and painted a white ring round its neck. All went well, until the vicar came for tea the next day, and the parrot called out,

'Oh, so they caught you at it too, did they, Vicar?'

99 In a monastery dedicated to prayer, Brother Gregory and Brother Alexander were discussing whether any indulgence of the flesh could be permitted. They both had a weakness for cigarettes, so they went to the abbot to ask his permission to smoke.

Brother Gregory went in and asked, 'Is it all right to smoke while I am praying?'

The abbot slapped him across the face and ordered him to do forty days' penance. Brother Alexander went in and—to the amazement of Brother Gregory—came out smiling.

'You mean, he didn't slap you and order you to do forty days' penance?'

'On the contrary,' said Brother Alexander, 'he congratulated me warmly!'

Brother Gregory was bewildered. 'How on earth did you manage that?'

'It's quite simple,' said the artful monk. 'You asked him whether it was all right to smoke while you were praying. I asked him whether it was all right to pray while I was smoking.'

100 Girl at confession: Father, I've committed the most terrible sin. I look into the mirror and I say to myself, 'Molly, you're the prettiest girl in all the world.'

Priest: Get away with you, Molly! That's not a terrible sin. That's just a mistake.

WISECRACKS

Wisecracks in this book are more than smart remarks. There is something illuminating about them which shines through the slick outer-casing of the wit.

101 'There's a good time coming, but it's a good time coming,' will say different things in different places.

Quoted by Bill Burnett, a former South African archbishop, it had a particular twist to it. Here are some other gems which, like diamonds, have a cutting edge.

102 There are only two reasons why we do things. The good reason and the real reason.

103 I can resist everything except temptation.
(Oscar Wilde)

104 It wasn't the apple that caused the trouble in the Garden of Eden, it was the pair on the ground.

105 You can't change the past but you can ruin a perfectly good present by worrying about the future.

106 A pessimist is someone who has lived with an optimist for too long.

107 Many a man aims at nothing and hits it with remarkable precision.
(Archbishop Whately)

108 If you are a Christian full of love, joy and peace, why don't you tell your face about it?

109 Every day people are straying away from the church and going back to God.

(Lenny Bruce)

110 The only exercise some people get is jumping to wrong conclusions, running down their friends, sidestepping responsibility and pushing their luck.

111 I believe in one Holy, Catholic and Apostolic Church, and I regret that it doesn't exist.
(Attributed to William Temple, former Archbishop of Canterbury)

112 Some ministers would make good martyrs: they are so dry they would burn well.

(C H Spurgeon)

113 If you showed me two roads, one to Hell and one to politics, I'd choose the one to Hell every time.

(Themistocles)

114 I must believe in the Apostolic Succession, there being no other way of accounting for the descent of the Bishop of Exeter from Judas Iscariot.

(Canon Sydney Smith, 1771–1845)

115 God made man in His own image—man has retaliated.

(Pascal)

116 To acknowledge you were wrong yesterday is simply to let the world know that you are wiser today than you were then.

(Dean Swift)

117 Resist the Devil and he will flee from you. Resist the deacons and they will fly at you.

118 Proverb aimed at moaning parishioners:
'The sheep who bleat will not be able to feed.'

HEAVEN

FIRMAMENT

EARTH

PURGATORY

OUTER DARKNESS

HELL

POLITICS

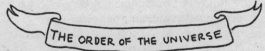

THE ORDER OF THE UNIVERSE

119 God so loved the world that he did not send a committee.

120 Hands off the Church of England! It's the only thing that stands between us and Christianity.
(MP in a Commons debate, quoted by Robert Runcie, Archbishop of Canterbury)

121 Carlyle said that men were mostly fools. Christianity, with a surer and more revered realism, says that they are all fools.

(G K Chesterton)

122 A puritan is a person who pours righteous indignation into the wrong things.
(Attributed to G K Chesterton)

123 I may have my faults but being wrong is not one of them.

124 Hospitality is the art of making people feel at home when you wish they were at home.
(Quoted by Lord Coggan)

125 She lived for others, and you could tell who the others were by the hunted look on their faces.

(C S Lewis)

126 Statistics can prove anything. If you put your head in the oven and your feet in the fridge, on average you'll be perfectly comfortable.

127 There is only one set of figures which cannot be manipulated to anyone's advantage: Death. It's the ultimate statistic. One out of one person dies.

128 For every difficult and complicated question there is an answer that is simple, easily understood and wrong.

(H L Mencken)

129 I've made up my mind. Don't confuse me with facts.

130 Some preachers who don't know what to do with their hands should try clamping them over their mouths.

131 Most people are bothered by those passages of Scripture they don't understand—but I have always noticed that the passages that bother me are the ones I do understand.

(Mark Twain)

132 A real Christian is a person who can give his pet parrot to the town gossip.

(Billy Graham)

133 Anybody can be Pope; the proof of this is that I have become one.

(Pope John XXIII)

134 Notice outside a church:
'Why pray when you can worry and take tranquillisers?'

HOT
UNDER THE
COLLAR

My great-aunt Ellie was an inspiration to me. She taught me—by example—that the church is really a collection of eccentrics. She was full of stories, usually about sex or faith-healing, or sex and faith-healing, which she would tell gleefully on unsuitable occasions. Sadly, I cannot remember any of these stories, only the stunned silence that followed them and the chink of bone china cups as people sipped tea and wondered how they could change the subject. I do remember her explaining to me why she—a 74-year-old widow—had turned up with yet another boyfriend.

135 'The light of my life went out, my dear, so I struck another match.'

She was a precursor of feminist theology:

136 'Man may be the head of creation, but it's the neck that turns the head.'

She used to regale us with stories about other eccentric Christians. One case I remember was about a woman she had come across who had decided to follow every prompting of the Holy Spirit on one particular day. Confusing irrational whims with guidance, she had changed her clothes three times before breakfast, kicked a neighbour's dog and jumped off a moving bus.

Of course, not everybody was eager to hear Aunt Ellie's endless flow of religious curiosities. After several hours of uninterrupted flow, one Boxing Day, she went into a lengthy spiritual analogy about the ocean which, although stormy on the surface, 'far, far below, deep down, there is a tremendous calm.' 'Yes,' said my father, who was feeling the burden of Auntie Ellie's company, 'and a tremendous pressure.'

My favourite story of hers was about an occasion when she was at a women's prayer meeting.

137 The old lady who was leading the meeting bent over to pray, and her wig fell off. She picked it up and put it back on, hoping that no one had noticed. However, after the prayer was over, everyone was staring at her in amazement. She had put her wig on back to front and she was smiling at them all, unaware that a large grey bun was sticking out of her forehead.

Here are one or two bizarre and several embarrassing incidents which would have received Aunt Ellie's warm approval.

138 A strange case was reported in the Daily Telegraph on February 27th, 1976. A vicar persuaded his housekeeper to help him rob a bank. He told her: 'It isn't wrong, because we're going to be like Robin Hood.' The defence explained that the Rev X, whose crimes netted £18,000, kept a Robin Hood outfit which he sometimes wore around the house—when he wasn't wearing a gorilla suit in the garden.

139 A minister was taking morning service when he suddenly realised that he'd left his car parked on double yellow lines at a dangerous corner. He couldn't think how to get out and move the car without an embarrassing interruption. Then it came to him—recently the church had been encouraging the congregation to join in the prayers and this was the perfect moment for a short period of 'open prayer'. He announced the prayers, then slipped out, unnoticed, to move his car.

The period of 'open prayer' went well, with many members of the congregation taking part, but it seemed to go on for a long time. After about 25 minutes, people became very restless and started to open their eyes. The vicar was nowhere to be seen. He had completely forgotten that he was taking a service and had driven home.

140 A young curate, trying to wake up his sleepy congregation, suddenly interrupted his sermon with the words, 'I remember the time when I was in the arms of another man's wife!' Everyone sat up. 'She was the wife of my father,' he added, to applause from the congregation. The bishop heard of this incident and decided that the joke would make an excellent introduction to his next

sermon. He stood up in the cathedral, before a vast congregation of Lord Mayor, town councillors and civic dignitaries.

'I remember the time when I was in the arms of another man's wife,' he began, with great aplomb. Then there was a long pause. The bishop stammered, 'Just for the moment, I can't remember whose wife she was!'

141 A vicar was having trouble with his microphone. The congregation could hardly hear him, but they followed the liturgy and dutifully gave their responses.

Finally, he sighed: 'There's something wrong with this microphone.'

'And also with you', came the response.

142 Like many free churches, a Baptist church in Nottinghamshire preferred to use non-alcoholic blackcurrant juice instead of communion wine. This, however, led to a bizarre incident one Sunday. The server realised that she had run out of Ribena and improvised by using blackcurrant jelly. She poured it hot and liquid into the cups, hoping that it would stay like that for an hour. When it came to the solemn moment, she hardly dared open her eyes. Hearing the sound of scraping, she looked up, and there, row upon row, were hundreds of people, reverently and prayerfully, trying to prise lumps of solid jelly out of their communion cups.

143 Several years ago, a Presbyterian minister was puzzled by the laughter which greeted his speech at a meeting of clergymen in Belfast. He stood up to voice the strongest protest against the emotionalism of the charismatic movement.

'I object,' he thundered, 'to all these feelings. All this playing on our feelings, stirring up our feelings, expressing our feelings. We hear far too much about feelings. Let me say,' he concluded, 'that I feel very strongly about this!'

144 An evangelist was about to speak to a very large audience when the Call of Nature compelled him to leave the platform. He knew there were about fifteen minutes before he was due to speak, and there were plenty of notices to be given out, so his presence would not be missed. As it happened, his presence certainly wasn't missed, because he forgot to switch his radio mike off.

145 The local priest was driving down a country lane in his Morris Minor when a Mercedes careered round the bend, spun out of control and crashed into the Morris. Both cars landed in the ditch. The driver of the Mercedes staggered over to the priest.

'By all the saints in heaven!' said the priest, 'you nearly killed me!'

'I'm sorry, Father,' apologised the man, taking a flask of whisky from his pocket. 'Here, have a drink of this, it'll calm your nerves.'

'Why there's more than an ounce of goodness in you, my son,' said the priest, taking a generous swig, 'to be sure, a drop of the old stuff won't go amiss at a time like this.' He took another gulp. 'Here,' he handed the flask back, 'have a swig yourself.'

'Oh, no, Father,' said the man, calmly, 'I'll just wait here till the police arrive.'

PIE
IN THE
SKY

146 I have been friends with Paul Burbridge, the Artistic Director of Riding Lights Theatre Company, all my life. When we were teenagers we went through a very pious phase. On one occasion, we had missed a bus to an important church meeting. We decided to kneel down by the side of the road, close our eyes and pray that God would send us another bus. As our eyes were shut, the bus went past.

A few years later someone pointed out to us that this would never have happened if we had followed the advice in the Bible to 'watch and pray.'

There's a difference between being a 'fool for Christ' and becoming a super-spiritual idiot. As they say, one can be 'too heavenly minded to be of any earthly use.'

These stories are intended for spiritual astronauts who are in need of a little training on the ground.

147 In 1842, a Roman Catholic priest wrote a book predicting that the world would end in 1847. On seeking the church's authority to publish the book, he was granted permission to publish it in 1848.

(Quoted in The Jesus Hope *by Stephen Travis)*

148 Overheard at a Christian conference:

    Man: I'm afraid I can't come to the meeting this afternoon, because the Lord has told me to go out and buy a toothbrush.

    Vicar: I hope the Lord has remembered to tell you that it's early closing day.

149 A boat crashed into rocks and began to sink. 'Does anybody know how to pray?' shouted the skipper.

'Yes, I do,' said a zealous Christian, leaping to his feet.

'Good,' said the skipper. 'You pray. The rest of us will put on life-jackets. We're one short.'

150 Members of the Elim church were getting carried away in worship. The tambourines were going, the drums were banging, the choruses were flowing in an everlasting stream and the prayers mounted to heaven like a thousand arrows loosed from the quiver. Amdist the sighs and shouts of joy, one old man was overcome with emotion.

'Oh dear Lord!' he called out. 'Thou canst see we're having a blessed time here tonight, Lord, but this is nothing, Lord. Thou shouldst have been at the meeting last Sunday, Lord!'

151 Did you hear about the religious family that took Sundays more seriously than anybody else? They took the swing out of the budgie's cage in case he enjoyed himself.

152 A lady came to a famous poet and handed him a piece of paper, explaining, 'The Lord has given me this poem'.

The poet scanned the appalling doggerel she had written, then screwed it up and threw it into the bin, with the reply,

'The Lord has given, the Lord has taken away, blessed be the name of the Lord.'

153 An evangelist was so successful, he converted his own horse. He decided to develop his ministry with animals and took his horse to the market, to exchange it for another. A farmer came riding along, on a very old horse, and the evangelist begged him to swap animals. The farmer looked at the fine fettle of the evangelist's horse and agreed, delighted with his bargain. As he mounted his new steed, the evangelist explained to him about the horse's religious zeal. The farmer looked at him incredulously.

'It's no good shouting "giddyup!" or "whoa, there, boy!"' the evangelist went on. 'To start, you have to shout, "Praise the Lord! Hallelujah!" and to stop, you have to shout, "Amen!"'

The farmer now realised that he was dealing with a nutcase, but he decided to humour him. The horse was in excellent condition and he accepted. As the evangelist trotted away on the farmer's ageing horse, the farmer shouted 'Giddyup thar!' to his steed. There was no reaction. He whipped the horse, but there was still no reaction.

'Go on tharr! Get going!' he screamed, digging in his heels. The horse refused to budge. The farmer scratched his head.

'Perhaps that old preacher wasn't so crazy after all,' he thought, 'oh, well, no harm in trying.' He took a deep breath and shouted: 'Praise the Lord, Hallelujah!' Immediately the horse galloped off. The astonished farmer clung on for dear life as it sped along the road.

'Whatever its religious quirks,' he mused, 'this is some horse!' On and on the pious creature went, crossing fields, jumping gates. At last, hearing the sound of the sea in the distance, the farmer knew that they were approaching the cliffs of Dover.

'Whoaa there, boy!' he called. 'Whoaa there!' He yanked the reigns. The horse sped on regardless. 'Silly me,' thought the farmer, 'I've got to say that special word!'

'Blessing!' he shouted. 'No, that's wrong. Faith!!' he called, urgently. 'No, that's not right either.'

The sound of the sea came nearer, and try as he might, the farmer could not remember the right religious word. Suddenly, within yards of the cliff edge, he remembered.

'AMEN!!' he screamed. The horse stopped, inches to spare. The farmer mopped his brow and, lifting his eyes to heaven in gratitude, murmured, 'Praise the Lord! Hallelujah!'

154 Speaker at a charismatic conference:
'Those who want coffee, hands down.'

155 Church of Scotland minister to Wee Free minister:
'I suppose we ought to have fellowship, since we are both about the Lord's business.'

Wee Free minister:

'Aye, mon, we're both about the Lord's business, you in your way and I in His.'

156 After a week of torrential rains, a river burst its banks and raged through a nearby village. Everyone grabbed planks or clung on to lampposts, and sooner or later they were rescued by life-rafts—all, that is, except for one very pious Christian who refused to come out of his house. 'The Lord will protect me,' he argued.

A naval officer drove a dinghy up to his front door, where the water was now rushing into his house.

'No, thank you,' said the Christian, climbing upstairs, 'the Lord will protect me.'

A lifeboat arrived hours later, as the river raged past the bedroom windows.

'No, really,' said the Christian, scrambling onto the roof, 'the Lord will protect me!'

As the waters lapped around the chimney, a helicopter whirred into sight and lowered a ladder.

'But you don't realise,' insisted the Christian, 'the Lord will protect me!'

Finally, the flood engulfed the house and the man was drowned. He arrived in heaven in a state of shock.

'But Lord,' he complained, 'why didn't you protect me?'

'I sent you two boats and a helicopter,' said the Lord, wearily, 'what more did you want?'

157 Scripture motto for the unbalanced Christian: 'So faith, hope and love endure, but the greatest of these is tongues.'

(from The Wittenburg Door*)*

158 The pastor of a Christian Science church was talking to a member of his congregation. 'And how is your husband today?'

'I'm afraid he's very ill.'

'No, no,' corrected the pastor, 'you really shouldn't say that—you should say that he's *under the impression* that he's very ill.'

The woman nodded meekly. 'Yes, pastor, I'll remember next time.'

A few weeks later, the pastor saw her again.

'And how is your husband at the moment?'

'Well, pastor,' she replied, 'he's under the impression that he's dead.'

MARRIAGE
LINES

Towards the end of the war, my mother was in charge of a Forces Welfare Centre in Belgium. On one occasion she tried to rescue a wedding which went disastrously wrong. The planning of the service was interrupted by an air raid. The bride forgot to buy any wedding shoes. There was no bridal car and she had to clamber into an armoured truck. Getting out of the truck, she slipped and sat on her wedding cake which was on the floor beside her. Just returning from buying the wedding shoes, my mother rushed off to the patisserie to persuade the local baker to patch up the devastated remains. Meanwhile, the congregation was baffled by the discrepancy between the hymns and the tunes played by the organist, and the vicar was in a state of shock.

After the service he rushed out, shouting, 'They're not married!'

'They must be!' said my mother, 'they've got to be!'

'No, no,' he cried, 'they've signed their names on completely the wrong pages in the register!'

Weddings and marriage are good for a laugh, usually a nervous laugh:

159 The humour probably goes back to the beginning of the human race. I am very fond of a cartoon which showed Adam and Eve expelled from the Garden of Eden, and Adam muttering to his wife: 'You and your vitamin C!'

Here is an introduction to courtship and marriage which has a few moments of relevance to the serious issues (but not many).

160 Kevin, a cockney lad, couldn't make up his mind which girl to marry. Sharon had blonde hair and blue eyes, Maria had black hair and green eyes. Sharon had a quick tongue, but she was funny, Maria was sweet-natured and serious. Over and over again he compared the two girls. The trouble was, both of them loved him and he loved both of them. One day, he was passing the Catholic church and, although he wasn't very religious, he decided in desperation to go in and pray.

'Oh God,' he cried, falling on his knees, ''Oo should I marry? I know I 'ave to make a choice, so 'elp me Lord. What d'yer say, Sharon or Maria, Maria or Sharon?'

Then the miracle occurred. He looked up and there above the altar, in letters of gold, was the advice: 'AVE MARIA'. So he did.

161 A woman who took her husband 'for better, for worse' found that he proved to be far worse than she took him for.

162 There is an ancient Jewish tradition that Jethro, the father-in-law of Moses, had seven names. The rabbinical explanation is that every time one of his seven daughters got married, he went bankrupt and changed his name.

163 A free-church clergyman was so scrupulous about his morals that he refused to perform any marriage ceremonies. His conscience would not allow him to participate in any game of chance.

164 How can a bishop marry? How can he flirt? The most he can say is, 'I will see you in the vestry after service.'

(Canon Sydney Smith)

165 Over a period of seven years, a young sailor taught his parrot to sing a hymn. When the bird was finally able to perform faultlessly, the sailor decided to invite the vicar and his daughters to tea. At first, the parrot was shy, but eventually, after a great deal of coaxing and many handfuls of birdseed, it sang the hymn before a delighted audience. Now confident, the remarkable creature sang the hymn twenty times, absolutely word-perfect. The vicar's family was so charmed that the sailor became a regular companion. One thing led to another, and eventually the sailor married the vicar's youngest daughter.

A year or so later, he accidentally wrung the parrot's neck.

166 Husband: But darling, yesterday you said I was a model husband.

Wife: Yes, and today I've realised that a model is a very small replica of the real thing.

167 We live in a two-story house. She's got her story and I've got mine.

(William Loblett Jnr)

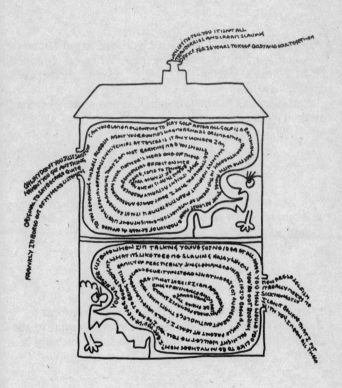

168 Prayer of a cricketer's wife:
'Oh Lord, if there is to be cricket in Heaven, let there also be rain!'

169 Eve was so jealous of Adam that when he came home each night she used to count his ribs.

170 A woman was infuriated by her husband's habit of leaving his socks on the floor. When he reminded her of Christ's teaching to 'forgive seventy times seven times', she replied:

'Well, just wait till the four-hundred-and-ninety-first time you do it, then!'

171 Inscribed on the tombstone of a husband and wife, married for 40 years, is the text: 'Their warfare is accomplished.'

172 Christian woman, trying to impress a feminist:
'My husband and I are completely equal in the sight of God, and I can assure you that my husband has given me full permission to say this.'

173 Martin Luther suffered from fits of depression. One day his wife came to him, wearing a black veil and a black gown. Luther was chastened, as she explained:

'I am mourning the death of God, for by the way you are behaving, God must surely be dead.'

PAINFULLY
AMUSING

174 While I was researching for a play about psychiatric abuse in the Soviet Union, I came across a story about an illegal prayer meeting in a Communist country. The secret police arrived and threatened the 20 or so Christians with arrest unless they denied their faith.

'Tell us that you don't believe in God and you can walk out of this door freely.'

Slowly, sheepishly, a number of people denied that they were true believers, and left. Finally, only six Christians remained. Their pastor turned to them, rubbing his hands enthusiastically:

'Now we can get on with the real business of this prayer meeting.'

The comment is both humorous and deadly serious.
Not all humour, emerging from extreme situations, is deliberate. Some of it reflects the absurdity of the system.

175 On my first visit to South Africa, I was looking for the toilets at Jan Smuts airport. I was so confused by all the signs saying 'Whites' and 'Non-Whites' that I went into the ladies.

On another occasion, an incident occurred which shows the absurdity of 'Christian' morality in the context of apartheid.

176 A white South African friend of mine heard rifle shots and ran out of his house. He saw two black schoolchildren being chased by soldiers. He grabbed one of the soldiers and started to argue with him. The soldier pushed him aside, he retaliated and they landed up fighting in the gutter. A crowd of white men gathered around, shouting comments, some supporting the soldier, 'Ja, man, you teach those kaffirs a lesson!' others disapproving of the soldier but refusing to become involved.

Suddenly, my friend's wife ran out of their house and started kicking the soldier, who swore very loudly. A man then stepped out of the crowd, slapped the soldier across the face and said, 'How dare you use language like that in front of a lady!'

Here are a few stories from behind the Iron Curtain, Northern Ireland, South Africa and Jewish communities.
Persecution, sectarianism, oppression do not stop at national boundaries, and fortunately neither does humour.

177 'The only difference between communism and capitalism is that with communism man exploits man, while with capitalism the reverse is the case.'

The idea of 'glasnost' or a more open society in the Soviet Union would have been unthinkable to Leonid Brezhnev. A few years ago a joke was circulating in Moscow about the former Soviet leader's attitude to reform.

178 Lenin, Stalin and Brezhnev are travelling on a railway train. Suddenly, the train stops. The guard enters and says, 'Terribly sorry to disturb you, comrades, but the train isn't moving.'

'Re-educate those who are responsible,' orders Lenin. The guard returns.

'Orders carried out, comrades, but the train still isn't moving.'

'Shoot the guilty ones!' screams Stalin. There is a burst of machine-gun fire. The guard returns.

'Orders carried out, but the train still isn't moving.'

'Paint the windows black,' says Brezhnev, 'and tell everyone we're moving.'

179 A black man is sitting on the doorstep of a white church in South Africa, weeping. Christ comes up to him and asks him why he is crying.

'They won't let me in.'

'I know exactly how you feel,' the Lord sympathises, 'I haven't been able to get in there for years myself.'

180 The Lord told a hard-line Protestant to go and work with Roman Catholics. The man refused, 'No, Lord, I don't agree with them.'

The Lord repeated, 'Go and work with the Roman Catholics.'

'No, Lord, I don't agree with them.' The Lord was persistent.

'But, Lord, you know that I just don't agree with those people!'

The Lord's gaze was piercing. 'Well, I don't agree with you, but I still want to work with you.'

181 A black church in the ghetto was so poor that the preacher sent round his hat for the offering. When it came back, it was empty. There was a pause. 'Thank you, my children,' said the preacher, 'for sending back the hat.'

182 A Rumanian asked for permission to emigrate to England.

'What's the matter?' asked the official. 'Hasn't the state given you a comfortable flat?'

'I can't complain.'

'Haven't you got a good job?'

'I can't complain.'

'Then why on earth do you want to emigrate to England?'

'Because there I *can* complain.'

> *(Told by Richard Wurmbrand,* In God's Underground,
> *Hodder & Stoughton)*

183 The Good Samaritan was tending the wounded Jew. He gave him a drink of water and mopped his brow. He poured oil on his wounds and bandaged them.

'Are you comfortable?' he asked him.

'Why wouldn't I be comfortable, with three shops?' said the Jew.

184 Advert outside a South African gun shop:
'For long life and good health, you need a gun.'

185 Paddy and Fergus were sitting in the pub having a drink with Mick. Somehow the conversation got round to the church and Paddy started insulting the Pope. Mick was furious. He picked Paddy up and threw him across the bar. There was a crash of bottles and the sound of moaning on the floor. Fergus leaned over the bar.

'By all that's holy,' he cried, 'did you not realise that Mick was a Catholic?'

'Sure I did,' replied Paddy, 'but how should I know the Pope was?'

186 A sign can be seen on a factory entrance in Northern Ireland: 'Religion stops at these gates. Christianity we allow in.'

187 A group of Russian Jews had gathered secretly for a Hebrew lesson. As they studied, the door burst open. A KGB officer stood there. He wandered silently around the room, taking down the names of the Jewish students. At last, he looked up from his notebook.

'Why are you learning Hebrew?' he asked them. 'What possible good is it to you? You'll never get to Israel!'

'Maybe,' said one of the Jews, 'but Hebrew is the language of Heaven and we're preparing ourselves to go there.'

'And what if you land up in Hell?' sneered the officer.

'Oh, that's all right,' answered another, 'we already know Russian.'

188 Advertisement in Ulster paper:
'Wanted—man and woman to look after two cows, both Protestant.'

189 Definition of religious prejudice:
A bingo hall where they call out the numbers in Latin, so only the Catholics can win.

190 The absurdity of violence was perfectly expressed by a 20-year-old in Northern Ireland. He said: 'When the last one of us faces the last one of them across the ruins of Belfast, the victory will go to the survivor.'

191 If anyone escapes violence from the armed forces in Soweto, or warring factions on the streets, there is still the danger of badly lit and pot-holed roads. All this produced a fine sense of priorities in one Sowetan. He was crossing the road, jealously guarding a bottle of wine under his coat, when a cab flew past and hurled him to the ground. He felt a trickle of dampness run down his chest. 'Oh God,' he prayed fervently, 'please let this be blood and not my wine!'

(Told by Mbuyiseli Deliwe)

192 A Jew named Goldberg was walking along the street when he was attacked by a thug.

'Why are you beating me?' he asked.

'For sinking the Titanic.'

'That wasn't my fault,' he protested, 'that was an iceberg.'

The thug hit him again. 'Iceberg, Goldberg, you're all the same.'

193 The Archangel Gabriel came to God. 'There's a man to see you.'

'Who is he?'

'He says his name's Epstein—claims to represent the Jewish people on earth.'

'All right, show him in.'

Epstein shuffled through the Pearly Gates. 'Lord, the Jews are wondering if you could answer one question?'

'Certainly. Go on.'

'Is it true that we are your Chosen People?'

'Yes.'

'We are definitely your Chosen People?'

'Yes.'

'Well, Lord, the Jews are wondering if you could choose somebody else for a change?'

194 Members of the Ku Klux Klan decided to hound a Jewish tailor out of town. They told their children to shout 'Jew! Jew!' outside his window. After several days of this, the tailor emerged and offered the children a dime, provided they went on shouting 'Jew! Jew!' all day.

The next day the children returned and began shouting abuse. This time the tailor came out and said that a dime was too much. He gave them each a nickel. The children were satisfied and carried on shouting.

On the third day, the tailor came out and gave them all a penny. The children complained.

'That's all I can afford,' replied the tailor.

'But two days ago you gave us a dime, then a nickel, now it's gone down to a penny. It's not fair!'

'That's my final offer,' said the tailor.

'Do you think we're going to shout "Jew! Jew!" all day for one penny?' shouted the children.

'So don't,' said the tailor. The children stormed off in a fury and never returned.

195 The Jewish prime minister was being entertained at the White House. In the president's office, he noticed a huge golden telephone, standing in an alcove under a soft light. 'What's that for?' he asked.

'Oh,' said the president coolly, 'that's our hotline to Heaven.'

'Direct to God?'

'Sure. It's our private line.'

The prime minister was intrigued. 'How much does it cost to make a call?'

'Well, about three thousand dollars a minute.' The prime minister whistled.

Later that year, the president visited Jerusalem. There, on the wall of the prime minister's office, was a huge silver telephone.

'What's that for?' asked the president.

'Oh,' said the prime minister, nonchalantly, 'that's my personal line to the Almighty.'

'I see,' said the president, a little nonplussed, 'and how much does it cost to make a call?'

'About fifty cents a minute.'

The president was staggered. 'Fifty cents! How did you arrange that?'

'Ah, well,' said the prime minister, 'it's a local call from here.'

THE
LAST LAUGH

A few years ago I visited Highgate Cemetery in London. There was a big banner announcing: 'Highgate Cemetery Open Day.' I was surprised by this, but then I suppose we all would be by the Last Judgement. I was waiting for the sound of the archangel's trumpet to boom over North London, when I was offered tea and biscuits by a Friend of Highgate Cemetery. My mind boggled even more. 'Open Day' at the cemetery, 'Tea and biscuits.' What next? 'Knock three times for sugar?' The simple explanation, the conservation of Victorian monuments, did nothing to quieten my fevered brain. Ever since then, the phrase 'Open Day' has been charged with a new and awesome significance.

Death requires a sense of humour. It is far too serious not to laugh about it. There is accidental humour, like the 'Open Day', and there is the deliberate wit of epitaphs and epigrams. One little touch is worth adding to the collection that follows. I saw an epitaph recently, in the United Reformed Church in Rectory Road, Hackney, which has to be read in a cockney accent:

196
In loving memory
Of my darling wife 'Lily'
Christiana: Louise: Adamson
Whose soul passed over to the Lord
On the 8th December 1952 and
Who worshipped in this church
With me Harry for
Many years

The hint of 'wiv me 'Arry' has a special place in my heart.

197 Death is nature's way of telling you to slow down.
(Graffiti)

198 Inscription on a tombstone:
'I told you I was sick.'

199 Due to industrial action, this cemetery will be maintained by a skeleton staff.
(Notice outside a cemetery)

200 Sacred to the memory of Major James Brush, who was killed by the accidental discharge of a pistol by his orderly, 8th of April, 1814.
'Well done, good and faithful servant.'

201 Two men were playing golf when a funeral procession passed by. One of the men doffed his cap reverently. His friend was impressed:
'It's nice to see you pay such a gentlemanly respect to the departed.'
'Oh, well,' said the other, selecting his number four club, 'she was a very good wife to me, you know.'

202 Mark Twain's obituary was accidentally published before his death. He cabled Associated Newspapers with the message:
'The report of my death was greatly exaggerated.'

203 The most dangerous thing in the world is living. There's a 100 per cent mortality rate.
(Quoted in a letter to the Daily Mail)

204 Emperors were divine, according to the official Roman religion, and were expected to join the immortals after death. As the Emperor Vespasian lay dying, he was heard to whisper: 'Oh dear, I think I'm becoming a god.'

205 The old churchyard has been sadly neglected, largely because there have been no burials there for more than 50 years. An appeal is to be launched to encourage volunteer bodies to remedy the situation.
(Quoted in the Peterborough Daily Telegraph)

206 Caption on a poster: 'The first two minutes of a man's life are the most critical.'
Graffiiti underneath: 'The last two are pretty dicey as well.'

207 We die only once, and for such a long time.
(Molière)

208 One of the crying needs of the time is for a suitable burial service for the admittedly damned.
(H L Mencken)

209 The famous Methodist minister, Dr Watkinson, was asked by two elderly ladies to provide a suitable epitaph for their beloved dog, who had departed this life and was to be solemnly interred in their garden. He wrote, suggesting: 'His barque is on the other shore.'

210 A wealthy person had died and the open-topped hearse drove slowly through the streets of the city. Suddenly, a lunatic broke from the crowd and jumped onto the coffin. One of the undertakers tried to pull him off, but the man was too strong for him, so he offered him £10 to come down. The man shook his head.

'£20.'

'Nope'.

A member of the family offered him £50 to come down.

'No, no.'

'All right,' said the wife of the deceased, '£100!'

'No,' said the lunatic, firmly. 'I'll open the box.'

211 Do not enter box unless your exit is clear.
(Ministry of Transport)

212 There is a tombstone in a churchyard in Bedale (Yorkshire) with the following inscription:

'Remember, friend, when passing by
As you are now, so once was I
As I am now, soon you will be
Prepare for death and follow me.'

Underneath someone has written:

'To follow you I'm not content
Until I know which way you went.'

213 Someone once described Jesus as 'The world's worst funeral director—he broke up every funeral he ever attended, including his own.'
(Denis Bennett in Nine o'clock in the Morning*)*

OUT OF THIS WORLD

I was sitting in a university canteen one day, during a spell as a visiting lecturer, when a physics professor tapped me on the shoulder. 'Did you have any idea,' he asked me gently, 'that the YMCA has been packed with people for the last half-an-hour waiting for you to give them a talk?' Later, I consulted my diary and discovered that one of the subjects I was going to talk about was 'Problems Facing the Writer'.

On another occasion, I went to the ticket office at Waterloo station and asked for a ticket to Waterloo. The man gave me a strange look and said 'Try again.' My mind went completely blank. I was just about to ask 'Well, what have you got?' when I remembered where I was going. I suppose this is the drawback of being a professional daydreamer.

214 Sometimes, I get so wrapped up in what I am doing that the world fades into oblivion. My most meaningful mental lapse was when I was writing a Christmas play. I had made the Archangel Gabriel a very important character and I had been thinking about him a great deal as I worked alone in my house. I went downstairs to make myself a cup of tea and, as I was taking the tray upstairs, I realised that I'd made two cups of tea—one for myself, and one for the Archangel Gabriel.

Perhaps this is what is meant by Hebrews, chapter 13, verse 2: 'Thereby some have entertained angels unawares.' I often wonder if the 'next world' is not so much the world 'after this one' but the world 'next door'. Heaven and Hell may be closer than we imagine. Normally, of course, we keep the 'hereafter' as far away from our thoughts as possible; it's an unpopular subject at cocktail parties, for instance; yet there is one very important exception to this rule. We are not so coy about eternity when it comes to telling jokes.

215 A golfer asked a famous mystic if there were any golf courses in Heaven. The old seer went away to meditate on the question. After many hours, he returned and said to the golfer:

'I have good news and bad news for you. First of all, the good news. There are many golf courses in Heaven, perfectly designed with the smoothest greens, supplied with immaculate equipment. Now the bad news. You'll be teeing off there at 10.30 on Wednesday.'

216 The abbot of a certain monastery spent his life denying the flesh. His life was not remarkable for what he had done, but it was certainly exceptional for what he had not done, and it was impossible not to be impressed by his extreme self-discipline. The novice monks looked up to him and, despite his somewhat cold and forbidding manner, found inspiration in his leadership. When he died, at an advanced age, he was spoken of with great reverence in the monastery. As it happened, a few years later, one of his most devoted disciples died and, arriving in the next world, saw the crusty old abbot with the most beautiful blonde on his knee.

'So this is Heaven!' said the monk, wide-eyed with envy, 'and I see you've got your reward!'

'Actually, this isn't Heaven,' said the abbot, 'and I'm her punishment.'

217 There was a door outside Heaven with a notice: 'ALL HEN-PECKED HUSBANDS QUEUE HERE.' A vast queue stretched to infinity. A few yards along there was another door with the notice: 'ALL HUSBANDS WHO HAVE LIVED IN PEACE AND CONTENTMENT QUEUE HERE.' One rather hunched little figure stood outside. The angel on duty came up to him.

'Why are you standing here?'

'I don't know really,' he laughed nervously, 'my wife told me to.'

218 Paddy arrived at Heaven's gate. St Peter shook his head. 'You're not on our list.'

'To be sure,' said Paddy, 'I don't know why that should be, sir.'

'I'm afraid I've been down all the O'Leary's and you're not here,' said St Peter, sorrowfully.

'Is there nothin' I can do then, your saintliness?' asked Paddy.

'It's too late now,' replied the Apostle. 'It's a question of what you've done in the past.' Paddy looked crestfallen.

'Look,' said St Peter, sympathetically, 'perhaps I can put in a good word for you. Have you ever done anything very good, for instance?'

Paddy looked more depressed. His mind was even blanker than usual.

'All right,' said the kindly saint, 'what about something really brave, perhaps?'

'Oh well,' said Paddy, brightening, 'I did once stand in the middle of the Falls Road and shout, "Down with all Catholics and Protestants!"'

'Remarkable!' said St Peter. 'When was that?'

'Oh, about thirty seconds ago.'

219 An old lady looked sternly at her naughty grandson. 'And what kind of children go to Heaven?'

'All the dead ones,' he replied.

220 A researcher asked a woman whose daughter had recently died what she supposed had become of her soul. The mother replied, 'Oh well, I suppose she's enjoying eternal bliss, but I wish you wouldn't talk about such unpleasant subjects.'

(Quoted by Stephen Travis in I Believe in the Second Coming of Jesus*)*

221 A man staggered up to the vicar at a Christmas party.

'Where the hell have I met you before?'

'I don't know,' replied the vicar with a smile. 'What part of Hell do you come from?'

222 A newcomer was being shown round Heaven. St Peter took him to a beautiful garden. There were Catholics and Methodists and Plymouth Brethren and Baptists and Anglo-Catholics and Presbyterians, all wandering around happily. Just then, they passed a huge, high wall and over the top floated the sound of a chorus being repeated endlessly.

'Who's in there?' asked the newcomer.

'Sssh!!' said St Peter, tiptoeing past. 'It's the charismatics. They're convinced they're the only ones up here.'

THE
FUNNY
SIDE OF
FAITH

223 I once met a man who told me that he had been converted to Christianity by going into a bookshop and seeing two books, side by side, *The Myth of God Incarnate* (a hardback) and *The Truth of God Incarnate* (a paperback). He could only afford the truth.

There is humour at the beginning of all Christian experience. It has been there ever since Christ casually asked two men on the road to Emmaus what had been happening in Jerusalem on the weekend of the Crucifixion. There's something very funny about that story. I particularly like the bit where the disciples recognise Jesus, he disappears, they run all the way to Jerusalem and are just about to tell the other disciples, when he appears again. It's a classic example of comic timing.

There are many contradictions in the Christian life, disappointments, surprises, delights, depressions, hopes and fears; but faith obeys the rules of comedy. All failures and absurdities are seen in the light of a happy ending.

Here are a few ups and downs along the way.

224 Parishioners arrived at their local church for Morning Worship to discover the doors locked and bolted. There was a notice from the vicar: 'You have been coming here long enough. Now go and do it.'

225

Mother: Son, it's getting late. You must get up and go to church!

Son: I don't want to go to church.

Mother: Give me two good reasons why you shouldn't go to church.

Son: First, I don't like the people. Second, the people don't like me.

Mother: I don't care. It's getting late, now get up and go to church!

Son: Give me two good reasons why I should go.

Mother: First, you are 50 years old, and second, you are the vicar.

226 A man was having coffee after a church service. The people around him were discussing the sermon on miracles and someone asked him, 'Do you believe that Jesus turned water into wine?'

'I'm only a beginner,' he said, 'I can't speak about water into wine yet, but in the few weeks I've known Christ, he's managed to turn beer into furniture and betting slips into groceries.'

227 A group of people huddled in a bus shelter during the war. The bombs fell dangerously close.

'Everyone pray!' ordered a Salvation Army captain. Each person prayed out loud, except for one.

'Pray!' shouted the captain.

'I—I—don't know any prayers,' faltered the man.

'You must know at least one.'

As the bombs screamed overhead, the man murmured: 'For what we are about to receive may the Lord make us truly thankful!'

228 Baptism has lost some of its significance in societies where it is fashionable to 'have the baby done'. The most extreme example of meaningless ritual was the case of a woman who arrived on the doorstep of the local vicar in Liverpool, handed him her baby and said, 'Please could you christen him while I do the shopping?'

229 Then there was the vicar who rolled up his sleeves, dipped his hands in the font and smiled reassuringly at the baptismal party, 'He should be in here somewhere.'

230 A minister was once asked how many active members he had in his church.

'They're all active,' came the reply, 'half of them are working with me and the other half are working against me.'

231 One insurance company in London is devoted to 'insuring churches against acts of God.'

232 Students of a famous theologian, who lectured all over the world, were exasperated at his continual absence. They pinned to a noticeboard the following axiom: 'The only difference between God and Professor Schultz is that God is everywhere and Professor Shultz is everywhere but here.'

233 Did you hear about the minister who wanted to move the church piano from the left hand side to the right hand side of his church? He knew that his congregation was violently opposed to change, so he worked out a plan. He moved it one inch every week for three years.

234 Someone asked a Christian woman about an incident which had wounded her very deeply. She looked blank. Her friend was astonished. 'But you were terribly hurt.'

'Well, I can't recall it.'

'But you must remember that!'

'No,' said the Christian firmly, 'I distinctly remember forgetting it.'

235 Men take a far less active part in the lay ministry of the church than women. Instead of 'Take my life and let it be', they prefer 'Take my wife and let me be.'

(Quoted by David Watson)

236 Two American tourists were travelling on a British train. One of them turned to his friend. 'See that guy over there? I'll bet you he's the Archbishop of Canterbury.'

'How much?' said his friend, unconvinced.

'Fifty bucks!'

'You're on, buddy!' The tourist got up and walked over to the stranger. 'Hey, sir,' he shouted in his ear, 'would you mind telling me—are you the Archbishop of Canterbury?'

'Mind your own—business,' the man replied, 'what the——has it got to do with you who I am?!!'

The American tourist returned to his seat and shook his head sadly. 'The bet's off. There's no way of finding out whether he's the Archbishop or not.'

237 Text above piano in a church hall:
'Do not let your left hand know what your right hand is doing.'

238 Notice outside a church:
'Services are at 11:00 and 6:30. Come early if you want a back seat.'

239 Overheard during a Christian mission:
'I was depressed earlier in the meeting, but now that it's finished I feel so much better.'

240 Martha, with her hard work in the kitchen, and Mary, who irritated her sister by sitting at the feet of Jesus and apparently doing nothing, are not simply two people of different temperaments but—according to medieval theologians—two types of Christian life. Martha represents the Active life, committed to good works, Mary the Contemplative life, committed to prayer and meditation. The 'Martha' and the 'Mary' schools of thought have often rivalled each other down the centuries for the position of the highest form of Christianity. One wise old preacher had the last word on the subject when he preached on the visit of Jesus to Bethany. 'I love them both,' he admitted, 'Martha before dinner and Mary after.'

241 Three Christians were discussing miracles.
'What are miracles?' asked the first.
'Well,' replied the second confidently, 'a miracle happens when God does exactly what our minister asks.'
'Really?' said the third. 'We think it's a miracle when our minister does exactly what *God* asks.'

242 Moses came down from Mount Horeb, holding the commandments he had been given by God. He gathered the children of Israel together.
'Right', he began, 'first the good news. I've managed to get them down to ten.' The people clapped.
'Now the bad news. Adultery's still in.'

243 Most people live their lives as if God gave man Ten Suggestions.

244 An old lady sat for hours watching her fish tank. Eventually, she turned to her husband. 'Same old rubbish,' she complained, 'nothing but sex and violence.'

245 The leader of a church music group practised his trombone till the small hours of every morning. Someone asked his vicar if such a man could be a good Christian. 'It's possible for the musician,' came the shrewd reply, 'but not so easy for his neighbours.'

246 A drunk was rolling around the street when the local minister came up to him.

'I'm so glad you've turned over a new leaf,' said the minister.

'Me?' said the drunk, amazed.

'Yes, I was so thrilled to see you at the prayer meeting last night.'

'Oh,' said the drunk, slowly remembering, 'so that's where I was!'

247 A young man was convinced of the truth of Christianity. Only one thing held him back from conversion: fear. He was paralysed with fear at the very thought of admitting to being 'a Christian', and the idea of telling anyone about his new-found faith, with all the dangers of being thought a religious nutcase, appalled him. For many weeks he tried to banish the thought of religion from his mind, but it was no use. It was as if he heard a tiny voice in his conscience, repeating over and over again, 'Follow me'.

At last, he could stand it no longer and he went to a very old man, who had been a Christian for the best part of a century. He told him of his nightmare, this terrible burden of 'witnessing to the light', and how it stopped him from becoming a Christian. The man sighed and shook his head.

'This is a matter between you and Christ,' he said. 'Why bring all these other people into it?' The young man nodded slowly. 'Go home,' said the old man, 'go into your bedroom alone. Forget the world. Forget your family, and make it a secret between you and God.'

The young man felt a weight fall from him as the old man spoke.

'You mean, I don't have to tell anyone?'

'No,' said the Christian.

'No one at all?'

'Not if you don't want to.'

Never had anyone dared to give him this advice before.

'Are you *sure*?' asked the young man, beginning to tremble with anticipation, 'can this be right?'

'It is right for you,' said the old man. So the young man went home, knelt down in prayer and was converted to Christ. Immediately, he ran down the stairs and into the lounge, where his wife, father and three friends were sitting.

'Do you realise,' he said, breathless with excitement, 'that it's possible to be a Christian without telling anyone?'

The Children's Society

Since its foundation in 1881, The Children's Society has aimed to help children and families facing deprivation and serious problems. The Society encourages community groups to tackle local needs; works in inner cities, on neglected housing estates, and in areas where there is a shortage of resources. By professional, pioneering, and Christian concern, the Children's Society demonstrates the wider Church's concern for thousands of children and families throughout England and Wales. Postal address: PR Dept, The Children's Society, Edward Rudolf House, Margery Street, London W1X 0JL. Tel: 01-837-4299.

Index

Numbers indicate joke numbers, not page numbers

Laughter in Heaven

Edited by Murray Watts

Fifteen superb sketches and a modern morality play from the Riding Lights Theatre Company.

The five contributors to this book share faith in Christ and a love of laughter. Both are infectious as the audience is drawn in to the drama, the fun and the inspiration.

'A valuable addition to the drama bookshelf'
Church of England Newspaper

'A good deal of bite'

Guardian

Murray Watts has established a reputation for innovative, fast-moving, and professional drama. Those who read and perform these Riding Lights sketches will not be disappointed.

128pp   £1.50

Playing with Fire

Edited by Paul Burbridge

Five Stageplays from the Riding Lights Theatre Company

Wherever the Riding Lights Theatre Company takes its plays, the cast is greeted with high acclaim. Paul Burbridge's selection of their plays in this book shows why.

Catwalk – Murray Watts portrays a prisoner of conscience in a Russian psychiatric hospital. Is he or is he not mad because of his faith?

St John's Gospel – Murray Watts' adaptation of the Gospel of John brings fresh insight to the familiar words.

A Winter's Tale – Nigel Forde travels with the Three Magi to show us the hilarious consequences of the gifts brought for the Christ Child – when the Magi meet the local customs officers and the camel has a mind of its own.

Promise – Andrew Goreing uncovers the anguish of a woman suffering from multiple sclerosis who seeks healing.

A Gentleman's Agreement – Murray Watts leads us through the hilarious escapades and misunderstandings of a group of undergraduates on the eve of their graduation.

Five full-length plays that will entertain, challenge and provoke.

256 pp   £3.95

One Stage Further

by Nigel Forde

In the tradition of Riding Lights Theatre Company's usual wit and polish, *One Stage Further* provides more entertaining and fast-moving sketches for performance by church groups and other amateur companies. Here Nigel Forde has written sixteen sketches and one full-length play, *Angel at Large*, to make us laugh, to make us think, and to make us want to change.

Doctor: It sounds as if you'd have done better to go to your dentist rather than come to me.
Rector: To a dentist?
Doctor: I think so, yes. I think what you've got there is a hollow truth. (Peers.) Just as I thought. There's a large truth here with a great, gaping hole in it. Too many sugary choruses...

'A collection of sketches on spiritual and moral themes that leap off the page with verve and wit.'
James Fox in his *Preface*

160pp   £1.95

Imagination: Embracing a Theology of Wonder

by Cheryl Forbes

First in the new series co-published by MARC Europe and the Greenbelt Arts Festival, exploring contemporary issues from a Christian perspective.

Imagination is the God-given ability of seeing life freshly. It helps us fill our lives with meaning. It is an energetic discipline, fuelled by the example of Christ himself. Cheryl Forbes, author of *The Religion of Power* shows us imagination at work in many different ways and many different people. Imagination, she shows us, empowers not only musicians and artists, but scientists, housewives, students, and office workers.

Cheryl Forbes teaches at Calvin College in Michigan. She has worked for both *Christianity Today* and Zondervan Publishing House.

Of this book *Publishers Weekly* said that it shows us how 'imagination can help awaken the transforming power of Christ.'

Co-published with the Greenbelt Arts Festivals

192pp   £2.50

Frogs and Princes

by Mike Starkey

Mike Starkey delights in and plays with the English language with the same reverence and wonder as a child delights in newly acquired words. He turns conventional views upside down to show us truth and make us laugh. With all the gutsy quality of good rock music, his lively, funny poems reveal Christian attitudes to the foibles of the world. His work is original, fresh, and thought-provoking.

Mike Starkey, though only in his early twenties, is already a well known poet. He reads his poetry all over the country and has received national and local media attention.

'This hilarious non-stop coconut shy...an undoubted talent'   ***Buzz***

the Princess is growing stranger since
she started searching for a Prince
the latest of her little fads
is sitting around on lily-pads

the King can never understand
(when so many princes want her hand)
rather than wearing her best glass slippers
she comes to dinner wearing flippers

Co-published with the Greenbelt Arts Festivals

96pp   £1.95